HOW TO HELP YOUR CHILD WITH WORRY AND ANXIETY

WELBECK
BALANCE

ABOUT THE AUTHOR

Lauren Callaghan (CPsychol, AFBPsS, PGDipClinPsych, PgCert, MA (hons), LLB (hons), BA) is a highly regarded clinical psychologist. She has worked at world-renowned research centres in London, UK, where she was recognized as a leading psychologist in the field of OCD, Body Dysmorphic Disorder and anxiety problems.

Lauren received further qualifications in systemic family therapy and uses her expert skillset to work with individuals and their families to overcome obsessional and anxiety problems.

HOW TO HELP YOUR CHILD WITH WORRY AND ANXIETY

Activities and Conversations for Parents to Help Their 4–11-Year-Old

Lauren Callaghan

WELBECK
BALANCE

A Trigger Book
Published by Welbeck Balance
An imprint of Welbeck Publishing Group
20 Mortimer Street
London W1T 3JW

First published by Welbeck Balance in 2021

A CIP catalogue record for this book is available from the British Library

ISBN
Trade Paperback – 9781789561982

Typeset by Lapiz Digital Services
Printed in Great Britain by CPI Group (UK) Ltd, Croydon CR0 4YY

10 9 8 7 6 5 4 3 2 1

Note/Disclaimer
Welbeck Balance encourages diversity and different viewpoints. However,
all views, thoughts, and opinions expressed in this book are the author's
own and are not necessarily representative of Welbeck Publishing
Group as an organization. All material in this book is set out in good faith
for general guidance; no liability can be accepted for loss or expense
incurred in following the information given. In particular, this book is not
intended to replace expert medical or psychiatric advice. It is intended for
informational purposes only and for your own personal use and guidance.
It is not intended to diagnose, treat or act as a substitute for professional
medical advice. Professional advice should be sought if desired before
embarking on any health-related programme.

www.welbeckpublishing.com

To all the children and parents who have experienced anxiety and been overwhelmed by worry, especially during the lockdowns of COVID-19.

CONTENTS

INTRODUCTION

It is great that you've picked up this book. It means you've taken a positive step toward your child's recovery from anxiety and worry.

I understand that, as a parent, it is very difficult to watch your child suffering from anxiety. Your immediate desire is likely to respond in a way that removes the anxiety completely. However, as you read this book, you'll learn that anxiety is, in fact, normal. It is nature's way of responding to a threat, and it prompts the 'fight, flight or freeze' mechanism (explained in more detail later), which is very useful in difficult situations.

> "You are by no means alone.
> Up to 10 per cent of all children
> experience anxiety problems."

If you're the parent of a child who is experiencing anxiety, you are by no means alone. Up to 10 per cent of all children experience anxiety problems. For most children, anxiety is only fleeting – a response to giving a talk in class or a trip to the dentist, for example. For others, it is a severe issue; a persistent, chronic problem that negatively affects many parts of their lives.

You may be unsure about how to help your child or how best to approach conversations about anxiety with them. You might have spotted some behaviours in your child that concern you or want to know the signs to look out for when anxiety begins to become a problem. This book will help you to navigate each of these roads and will provide a stable companion as you and your child tackle their worry and anxiety together.

> "Please do not blame yourself
> if your child experiences
> problems with anxiety."

TIP

It is normal, as a parent, to feel guilty for the part you think you have played in causing your child's anxiety.

However, please do not blame yourself. It is not helpful for you or them, and it won't help your child overcome it.

Anxiety problems develop for many reasons and they are very common. The best thing you can do is decide to help your child overcome their anxiety problem.

WHAT ARE WORRY AND ANXIETY?

In simple terms:

Worry is when we dwell on things that we believe are threatening to us in some way. We keep thinking about these things and may go over and over them in our heads. Worry is usually based on things that haven't actually happened, so we often worry about what 'might' happen.

Another type of problem associated with worry is when we can't stop thinking about things that have happened in the past, and we go over and over them in our head, causing us to feel anxious and upset. These past events are usually unpleasant experiences and can lead to worry about them happening again.

Anxiety is a physical and emotional response to worry – to something we consider to be threatening. We all experience anxiety at some point in our lives. When we feel anxious, this affects how our body responds, known as the 'fight, flight or freeze' response. This is a very human, very normal way of responding when we feel under threat.

The words 'anxiety', 'fear' and 'worry' are often used interchangeably, but here are the definitions of how I use these terms in this book:

- **Worries** are the thoughts we have about a future event, real or imagined, that scare us. Or they can be about things that have already happened that we can't change.
- **Fear** is the emotional reaction to real or perceived imminent danger.
- **Anxiety** describes the emotional and physiological sensations that we have in response to what we anticipate as a threat.

UNDERSTANDING ANXIETY

Anxiety is a perfectly natural response to threatening situations, and we all experience it from time to time. It is a fundamental part of being human; we cannot banish it permanently just because at some points in our lives it misfires and becomes a problem. What we can do instead is manage it so that it doesn't become a bigger problem than it needs to be.

"It is only by *understanding* anxiety and worry that your child will ever learn to *manage* them, and stop them severely impacting their life."

The biggest lesson to teach your child is not to fight or run away from worries. Instead, they should know them for what they are, accept they are a normal part of life, and by doing so, learn to manage them.

Children who experience troubling or anxious thoughts can feel incredibly weighed down, isolated and confused. It is only by *understanding* anxiety and worry that your child will ever learn to *manage* them, and stop them severely impacting their life.

Think about it like jumping off a diving board. At first, the fear you have as you stand above the drop feels overwhelming, but then you jump and realize that it wasn't quite as bad as you thought it was going to be. Then you do it again, and again, and each time you do it, you feel less and less fear.

That is how you can help your child tackle anxiety and worry – by taking steps to face it and accepting some level of fear. Following this approach will give your child everything they need to reduce the negative impact of the worries and fears that could dominate their life.

> "In helping your child learn skills to manage anxiety, you are giving them important building blocks for good future mental health."

If you help your child recognize anxiety and encourage them to learn skills to manage it so it doesn't become a problem, you are giving them important building blocks for good future mental health.

Everyone experiences stressors in life at different points, so gaining the skills needed to navigate worry and anxiety at an early age provides the resilience and knowledge to face such situations effectively in the future.

THE APPROACH USED IN THIS BOOK

In this book, you will learn what anxiety and worry are, and how you can help your child develop strategies to help manage them. Your child will not be encouraged to *battle* or *fight* with their difficulties, because that does not work.

The treatment within this book is a combination of Cognitive Behavioural Therapy (CBT) with a Kindness-Focused Approach, but tailored for children and young people.

Some things to note about CBT:

- It is the most evidence-based treatment available, backed up by years of research.
- It provides a new way of examining unhelpful thoughts.
- It helps look at thoughts in a different way and encourages people to change their unhelpful responses to anxiety-provoking situations.
- It gets easier the more it's done.
- It is meant to give the user the tools to keep good mental health so they can use them whenever they feel anxious or stressed.

The Kindness-Focused Approach is one that encourages you to use the strategies and skills from CBT, but with compassion for yourself and your child.

By learning to be non-blaming, non-judging and kind to themselves, children learn self-compassion – something that is necessary to be a happy, successful adult.

When you're concerned that your child's anxious thoughts and worries are taking a toll on them, the last thing you need is a lot of confusing information. I aim to show you a simple approach that helps.

> "Everyone has unhelpful thoughts, uncomfortable feelings and strange or problematic behaviours from time to time."

It is also important to remember that everyone has unhelpful thoughts, uncomfortable feelings and strange or problematic behaviours from time to time. While it's normal for children to experience worry and anxiety, I want to give children tools to overcome their anxiety when it feels overwhelming.

Showing your child the techniques they need to break the chains of anxiety gives them the opportunity to use them throughout their childhood and teenage years. The aim is to give them tools and tips that will help them for many years to come.

> **TIP**
>
> Following this approach might seem uncomfortable at times, but it can create very real results.

HOW TO USE THIS BOOK

This book will help you understand what anxiety is and how it applies to your child. Work though each section and activity carefully.

The activities are specifically designed for parents and carers to do *with* your children, together, and involve discussion topics, conversation scripts and fun tasks to be done in collaboration.

Hopefully, this will open a two-way conversation about your child's anxiety, so that a previously difficult or hard-to-talk-about topic can be aired and worked through, surrounded by support, encouragement and care.

Such involvement and investment can be a big ask when you have busy working lives and possibly other children in your care, but if you can devote just a bit of time every week, you'll soon see the benefits.

Think about it like another school lesson: 15–20 minutes a week (or, ideally, a few times a week) for improving wellbeing and mental health. This approach is not complicated, but it does require some commitment. As a parent, you will need to be your child's guide.

> "The exercises will open a two-way conversation about your child's anxiety, so that a previously difficult topic can be worked through together."

Part 1 will set out what anxiety is and how it manifests in children. It gives advice about how to recognize the first signs of worry and anxiety in your child, details common symptoms of anxiety-related disorders within children, and looks at the thought processes that your child might experience. In Chapter 4 we will also look further into why normalizing and accepting rather than fighting thoughts is the best approach.

Part 2 introduces the CBT-based approach to help your child understand and manage their anxiety. Through the activities, your child will begin to see the connections between their worries, how they feel and what they're doing (or not doing) to make them go away.

Chapter 5 begins with the four building blocks of helping your child – ensuring you are approaching the situation in the best way possible.

> "Your child will begin to see the connections between their worries, how they feel and what they're doing (or not doing) to make them go away."

Chapter 6 gives you a number of activities to try with your child, focusing on thinking activities that invite self-reflection and imagination as a way of dealing with anxiety, as well as looking at thinking traps that cause anxiety, and how these can be avoided.

Chapter 7 gives you activities that you can do 'in the moment' with your child, if they are particularly struggling with worry, encouraging a calm mind or providing a distraction.

YOUR ROLE

It is important to consider your behaviour around a child with anxiety problems, and how not dealing with it in the right way can make the anxiety much worse.

I encourage you to think about how your child's anxiety is affecting patterns of family life, how you might be facilitating this and how to manage it for the benefit of everyone.

For example, there is no need to make an anxiety disorder the whole family's problem, or restrict what the family does socially as this gives the anxiety problems more significance in family life than they deserve.

It might be difficult for you to engage with this treatment plan if you also suffer from anxiety yourself, because you want to protect and reassure your child about the things they find distressing (which might be things you find distressing, too).

Again, this is perfectly normal and should not be a reason *not* to try this approach. If this is something you recognize in yourself, I would encourage you to seek help for your anxiety.

If your child sees you being brave and taking steps to overcome your own problems, they will be more likely to model this behaviour.

YOU KNOW YOUR CHILD BEST

One of the most important things to remember when going through this book and its activities, conversation scripts and tips is that *you know your child best*.

> "Your 'insider' knowledge about how your child functions is crucial."

This 'insider' knowledge about how your child functions is crucial and should be used to adapt every activity to suit your child, or to pick-and-choose the right ones for them. Even so, I would encourage trying different activities, as children enjoy trying a variety of approaches. Every child is different and this should be accommodated by the parent as much as possible.

With that in mind, care should also be taken to make any of the content or conversations fitting for your child's particular age within the book's age range of 4–11 year olds. Consider your child's emotional intelligence, and the kind of language that you usually use day to day.

EXTRA HELP

I completely understand that dealing with anxiety is scary and difficult, and that serious anxiety problems might be more than you can manage at home, but there is help out there.

Your child may need extra help from a professional like a psychologist, child specialist therapist or a child psychiatrist. Please speak to your child's school or doctor about the next steps.

If your child reacts well to the CBT techniques throughout this book, you may want to consider a formal diagnosis and individual CBT treatment with a suitably trained professional.

See also the Useful Resources at the back of the book.

SWITCH YOUR PERSPECTIVE

While it can be heartbreaking to see your child struggling with worries, another way of looking at it is that it's possible to make working on our mental health the biggest *positive* influence in our life.

If approached correctly, our mental health problems can actually give us the platform we need to take action and create a fulfilling life for the future. Indeed, learning about our mental health can give us a strength and resilience we did not know we had.

> "If approached correctly, learning about our mental health can give us a strength and resilience we did not know we had."

It won't always be easy. It is challenging and it requires patience, perseverance and trust. However, if you approach this book and treatment method with an open mind, you will see results, even when it feels like the opposite.

THE EFFECT OF COVID-19 ON CHILDREN'S MENTAL HEALTH

Whilst writing an advice-led book to help parents work with their children on their anxiety, the world was plunged into a new and anxiety-provoking situation in the form of the COVID-19 pandemic. This created intense anxiety for everyone – children and adults alike.

We moved through the pandemic and the lockdowns that seemed to last forever, social isolation, the pressures of homeschooling and working from home, financial and job insecurity, and the worry about contracting COVID-19 or passing it on to others, all the while not being able to see our extended family, grandparents, friends, teachers, and other important support people. The effect on children's lives was immense.

The UK's Ofsted chief inspector Amanda Spielman rightly described in January 2021 that when you close the schools, you "put children's lives on hold".

Understandably there has been a predictable rise in reported anxiety amongst children (and adults) – and research is ongoing into the lasting effects of COVID-19 on our mental health.

> "I have been amazed at our children's resilience during the COVID-19 pandemic, and their ability to adapt to the changed world."

If you believe your child's anxiety has increased or sprung from the effects of the pandemic, please know the information and strategies in this book are very relevant to you, and can be used despite the changed environment.

Overall, I have been amazed at our children's resilience during this period and their ability to adapt to the changed world. I believe that we can overcome both this collective anxiety, and the individual-level anxiety created by the pandemic, and work together to a better, healthier way of thinking.

Good luck on your and your child's journey!

Lauren

PART 1

UNDERSTANDING YOUR CHILD'S WORRIES AND ANXIETY

CHAPTER 1

ABOUT ANXIETY

"Anxiety is normal and we all have worries.
Anxiety can become a problem
when you experience it too frequently
or intensely, and it causes you
to feel distressed."

Anxiety, far from being a problem, is actually a *normal human reaction* to something we perceive as a threat. For example, if we're out walking and see a big dog running toward us, barking loudly, we're likely to react in two ways:

- The first is our emotional reaction, which would usually be *fear*.
- The second is our physical reaction. We might sweat, feel our heart start to race and become jittery.

No matter that the dog might run past and pay us no attention; we respond instinctively to what we perceive as a threat. This is our 'fight, flight or freeze' response kicking in. So, what do we do next?

- **Fight** – do we stand our ground and hope the dog backs off?
- **Flight** – do we run away before the dog reaches us?
- **Freeze** – do we stay still, hoping that the dog runs past and doesn't notice us?

WHAT IS FIGHT, FLIGHT OR FREEZE?

"The prehistoric survival response of 'fight, flight or freeze' has stayed with us to the present day."

The 'fight, flight or freeze' response has its roots in prehistoric times, when early man faced dangerous predators that would kill him for food if they got the chance. As we evolved, we kept this basic survival response and it has stayed with us to the present day.

When we're faced with some kind of a threat, we get the same surge of adrenaline that early man experienced – that's what makes us feel brave and gives us the extra strength to fight, or the extra speed to run away, while the freeze response stops us drawing attention to ourselves, thus hoping the predator goes on their way.

TIP

Fight, flight and freeze is a wonderful tool – a protective response to help keep us safe.

There's just one problem. Fight, flight or freeze makes more sense when the threat is very obvious in our environment. A big dog running toward us has the potential for threat. An even more obvious threat was the prehistoric sabre-toothed tiger prowling around outside a cave – so the cavemen inside either hid or agreed to join together and fight it off.

Today, threats aren't always so obvious. As well as physical threats, such as the dog or sabre-toothed tiger, threats can be mental and emotional, too. And though we respond to the threat in the way we always did, with 'fight, flight or freeze', it can be harder now to pinpoint exactly *what* that threat is.

> "Threats aren't always obvious.
> They can be physical, but also mental
> and emotional."

For example, a child answering a question in class or encountering a negative comment in the playground could cause as much anxiety, relatively speaking, as the sabre-toothed tiger did to our cavemen ancestors. It won't kill you, of course, but it is a threat in today's world, because:

- Being rejected or made fun of is a challenge to your child's social standing.
- It might cause your child to become shy or withdraw from friends.
- It might make your child under-perform at school.
- It may make your child worry about what people think of them.

These responses are perfectly normal because *anxiety is normal and everyone experiences it*, even those who seem to be so calm on the outside.

WHEN DOES 'NORMAL ANXIETY' BECOME A PROBLEM?

So, anxiety is normal and we all have worries – even those who seem confident.

Worry and anxiety can become a problem when you experience it too frequently and/or intensely, and it causes you to feel distressed. Your 'threat-interpretation system' isn't managing your threat response as well as it should.

This happens when:

- You misinterpret something as a threat when it is benign.
- You estimate the risk of a threat disproportionately (in that you think it is much more likely to occur than it is in reality).
- You believe that the consequences of the threat will be disastrous and unmanageable.

> "For those with anxiety, their thoughts suggest a threat is imminent. This triggers a fear response."

People without anxiety only pay attention to the thoughts they feel are important, like remembering to buy a birthday card or deciding which pair of shoes to buy. However, for others with anxiety, their thoughts are ones that suggest a threat is imminent. It triggers a fear response, leading the person to behave in certain ways to try to get rid of those thoughts and feelings, or to stop the thought (a worry) from coming true.

It might stop you from doing things you used to enjoy, or stop you visiting places you used to like going to. And when you think about your worries a lot, they appear to grow bigger and bigger.

"Research has shown that children with anxiety problems do not think about *different* types of threats more than children without anxiety problems, but they think about them *more frequently*."

We all have thoughts that signal a threat of some kind. We have to review information in our environment and sift out threatening situations in order to react and stay safe.

Someone with an anxiety disorder would interpret the information as more threatening than it is (overestimate the likelihood of threat) or believe there is a threatening situation when there isn't one (catastrophizing).

So, all anxious thoughts are normal; in the sense they are interpretations of threat. But what is *not* normal is the extent to which we believe a threat is imminent or likely, or even when we believe non-threatening situations portray a threat.

DIFFERENT INTERPRETATIONS OF THE SAME THOUGHT

Claire and James are in the same class at school and have to make a presentation about someone famous.

Claire is going to talk about her favourite athlete and thinks everyone will be interested in what she has to say. She feels positive and excited about the presentation and when she gives it, the class sits up and takes notice. Afterward she is praised by the teacher for her confident manner.

James, on the other hand, is not looking forward to the presentation. He has chosen to talk about his favourite sports player, but he thinks no one will be interested. This makes James feel nervous, sweaty and anxious. He thinks everyone will laugh at him. When it's his turn to stand up, he makes an excuse that he feels ill and is sent to see the school nurse. He never makes the presentation and, even in years to come, is anxious about any kind of speaking in public.

Here are two people in exactly the same situation, but with very different responses.

> Do you see the link between their thoughts, feelings, physiological responses and behaviour?
>
> James *thought* no one would be interested in his presentation. He interprets the situation as being a threat to him socially, so he *feels* nervous and has a physiological response in his *body* – becoming sweaty and panicky. His *behaviour* is to avoid the situation by making an excuse that he is ill.

No two people think about, or respond to, the same situation in exactly the same way. You might climb a steep rock face with no fear at all, but break down in tears when you find a small spider in your bedroom.

> ## "How *we think about* and *interpret* a situation is the key factor in how we *respond* to it."

Conversely, you may handle a large spider without any worries, but feel sick and dizzy standing at the bottom of the cliff.

How we *think about* and *interpret* a situation is the key factor in how we *respond* to it. This is something we will cover in the activities in the book, and look to teach your child how to think about and interpret situations differently.

ANXIETY IN CHILDREN

All children will experience worry and anxiety – it's a perfectly normal part of a child's development and it helps them to develop the skills they need to deal with situations that worry them. For children, common worries might include:

- performance at school
- relationships with friends
- health fears/dying
- losing people close to them.

The focus of children's worries change as they get older. Younger children experience very immediate threats relating to their own survival, so may experience a fear of loud noises or strangers.

"Anxiety starts to become a problem when it interferes in your child's life in some significant way."

As they get older, their fears may progress to losing caregivers. It may centre on a fear of rejection from friends. Rejection can mean loss of social status or being part of a group – something that has been central to our survival instinct as a species.

Research has shown that children with anxiety problems do not think about *different* types of threats more than children without anxiety problems, but they think about them *more frequently* and find them harder to dismiss.

Children with anxiety share many similar concerns as their peers, including worries about schoolwork, friendships, personal harm and disasters, but their experience of anxiety varies in its intensity and how much it interferes in their lives.

Children with anxiety problems can experience severe, chronic and intense anxiety, which can be debilitating.

Anxiety starts to become a problem when it interferes in your child's life in some significant way. This could be their performance and attendance in school, or in sports and leisure activities, or it might hinder their attempts to make friends or socialize.

> **TIP**
>
> If your child does suffer from an anxiety problem, it is unlikely to get better on its own without help.

If you feel your child might have fears and worries that are not normal for their age range (see Chapter 2), it will be worth talking to teachers or learning mentors at their school to see if they've noticed anything relating to their learning, socializing or general behaviour.

HOW DO WORRY AND ANXIETY IN CHILDREN START?

As a parent, you might ask yourself, 'How did these worries and anxieties start, and why?' It's an interesting question and it's important to say that we don't need an answer to treat them. That said, sometimes it's useful to know some reasons, especially if you're helping a child through a treatment approach like this one.

The situations in which your child experienced anxiety in the past may now trigger *worry* – that is anticipatory anxiety of a similar event happening again.

If a barking dog running toward us has caused us anxiety, we might start to worry about what will happen next time we encounter *that* dog. And we might extend this to worry about what will happen the next time we see *any* dog. So, the worry has grown from a simple response to a barking dog into one that takes in all dogs, barking or not.

"You don't need to know exactly why your child get anxious to start helping them."

Similarly, if children encounter a negative experience in the playground, they interpret it as a threat in their social world and it can cause great anxiety. They start to worry about what people think about them and dread receiving more negative comments, which makes them shy away from social gatherings and other social encounters.

> "Take on the responsibility of giving your child the opportunity to develop the skills they need to build confidence and future resilience."

Research suggests that worry and anxiety are the result of a combination of several factors, including:

- Genetics.
- Individual and personality traits.
- External situations – for example, a run-in with a dog in the park might lead to a phobia of all dogs.
- Modelling behaviour, in which a child copies the behaviours of those around them, especially his caregivers.

While we can't always pin down exactly why someone has developed an anxiety problem, it doesn't help if a caregiver blames themselves. If you have your own problems, seek help and set a good example for your child. Don't blame yourself for your child's problem, as this may prevent you from seeking help for them. Instead, take on the responsibility of trying to set your child on the right path and give them the opportunity to develop the skills they need to build confidence and future resilience.

TIP

Remember: we all have moments of anxiety. It is when those moments become frequent and life-affecting that we consider anxiety a problem.

Life experiences can also play a role in childhood anxiety. Disorders can develop after a traumatic event or there can be anxiety already in the family, which a child models their behaviour on.

If a parent is nervous about spiders and does everything to avoid them, it's no surprise that their child might do the same. However, it's not inevitable that a child will develop the same problem as their caregiver, or any anxiety problem at all.

TIP

If you are a parent and you're anxious, it's worth speaking to someone qualified about this and how you might work through it in order to help your child.

FIRST SIGNS OF WORRY OR ANXIETY

It can be difficult to pinpoint when worry or anxiety begins to be a problem, but there are certainly signs to look out for, some of which are listed below.

Please note that if your child experiences only one of the signs occasionally, it may not be due to an anxiety problem. However, if several signs are present, consistently, take note and take action.

First signs:
- Irritability
- Tearfulness
- Somatic complaints, such as stomachache or headache
- Avoiding friends or other social situations
- Reluctance to go to school
- Avoidance of specific things or situations
- Clinginess
- Withdrawal
- Moodiness
- Trouble sleeping

SYMPTOMS OF ANXIETY

You may have already noticed changes in your child's behaviour at home, and noted that your child experiences several of the symptoms in the box above. Consider:

- Are they avoiding things they used to like doing?
- Are they moody, tearful or clingy?
- Are they spending more time on their own?

Remember that it might be hard to distinguish symptoms of anxiety from normal development – not every change in behaviour is down to an anxiety problem!

However, if the changed behaviour turns into a pattern, or you just can't decide which is which, it will be worth asking questions of your child to discover how they're feeling and establish if anything is worrying them. You might get a vague response ('I'm fine' and 'Nothing's wrong'), but if your instinct tells you that something is up and it isn't being said, keep trying.

An anxiety problem that goes undiagnosed and untreated often continues in various ways for years, affecting your child's life into adulthood.

"Note the symptoms your child experiences, to start building a picture of your child's anxiety experience."

Children and young people may show a variety of symptoms if they have an anxiety problem. Opposite is a list of common symptoms of anxiety in children, though it is not exhaustive.

Don't worry if your child shows a different collection of symptoms or worrying behaviour.

- Intense feelings of fear
- Difficulty concentrating
- Irritability
- Unwillingness to take part in activities
- Refusing to speak
- Shrinking away from the situation
- Refusal to leave main caregiver or leave the home
- Freezing when the situation or object of fear is encountered
- Excessive clinginess
- Difficulty sleeping
- Nightmares
- Tiredness
- Nausea or sore stomach
- Muscle aches
- Chest pains
- Crying
- Having tantrums
- Sweatiness
- Light-headedness
- Headaches
- Shaking

It's very possible that your child has a problem with anxiety – you've noticed behaviour that has made you buy this book, for one. Note the symptoms your child experiences, to start building a picture of your child's anxiety experience. Note that many of these symptoms overlap, and a child may experience one or more of them.

> "Every child is unique, and has a different way of showing anxiety. Trust yourself and your instinct, because you know your child best."

If you do not recognize symptoms of your child's anxiety from the list of symptoms, it doesn't mean they're not experiencing anxiety of some kind and that it is not interfering in their life.

Every child is unique, and has a different way of showing anxiety. Some will internalize and keep it to themselves, whilst others will externalize – that is, clearly showing it with their behaviour in some way. Trust yourself and your instinct, because you know your child best.

COMMON ANXIETY DISORDERS

Children develop quickly, so pinning them down to one diagnosis is not always easy or, indeed, helpful. It is also common for children who have problems with anxiety to meet the criteria for more than one anxiety disorder. A list of anxiety disorders is below for reference. Please view this as a general guide only and seek professional advice if you want to get a formal diagnosis for your child. Many children can improve their experience of worry and anxiety without the need for a formal diagnosis.

"Children with generalized anxiety disorder are often referred to as 'worriers'."

GENERALIZED ANXIETY DISORDER

A person worries excessively about a range of different things and feels they cannot control these worries. Children tend to worry about school and sporting performance, punctuality and catastrophic events. These worries can interfere with the child's ability to enjoy activities at home, at school or with friends. Although it is not often diagnosed until adulthood, children can have this disorder and they are often referred to as 'worriers'.

SEPARATION ANXIETY DISORDER

Worries, fears and anxieties around separation from parents, carers or other people to whom the child is attached. It can also be around places, although children usually worry about being away from home. Children will worry about people close to them dying or being harmed in some way, or think about something bad happening to them (getting lost, being kidnapped) that results in them being separated from a major attachment figure. Specific symptoms of this disorder are: reluctance to leave home or go anywhere due to fear of separation, nightmares about separation, and refusal to sleep away from home, or go to sleep without the main caregiver at home. Worry around losing parents or caregivers is common in childhood, but if it is causing real interference in the child's life and the symptoms last for more than four weeks, it's likely that it requires more specific help.

SOCIAL ANXIETY DISORDER

Social anxiety disorder is the fear of embarrassing yourself in front of your peers. Up to 75 per cent of cases begin between the ages of eight and 15. For a diagnosis of SAD, symptoms must last for six months or more, and the fear of being embarrassed or ashamed will be disproportionate to the actual threat. Like all anxiety disorders, not treating it can cause significant difficulties in later life.

SPECIFIC PHOBIAS

Strong fears and anxieties about certain objects and situations (e.g. dogs, spiders, heights, water, the dark, loud noises, strangers, aeroplanes, blood, vomit, etc.). A phobia lasts for at least six months and the fear is disproportionate to the danger posed by the object or the situation. For example, a child with a phobia of water will refuse to go near a park with a lake or may become distressed when passing the beach in a car.

PANIC DISORDER

Panic attacks are intense feelings of anxiety that come on quickly and are extremely unpleasant. The sufferer will worry about having reoccurring panic attacks and will go out of their way to avoid the possibility of this. Panic disorder is less common in children, but may occur in adolescents.

OTHER ISSUES

Anxiety can also manifest as selective mutism – an ongoing failure to speak in certain social occasions where the child would normally be expected to speak, for example, at school or family events – or agoraphobia – the fear of being in a specific situation and not being able to escape or find help if a panic attack, or other symptoms, occur.

Children may fit into more than one disorder at the same time, but it's common to cross over different diagnoses. For example, a child might meet the criteria for social anxiety disorder and selective mutism. As clinicians, we treat these diagnoses as guides rather than a set of criteria to be religiously ticked off.

OBSESSIONAL PROBLEMS

I also need to mention obsessional compulsive disorders which are often characterized by anxiety and worry. These disorders used to be classified under 'anxiety disorders' but are now in a category of their own. Disorders in this category include:

Obsessive compulsive disorder (OCD): A problem defined by having excessive and unwanted obsessional thoughts which cause distress and compulsions, rituals or other behaviours to try to stop or 'undo' the thoughts or prevent the feared outcome, or any other repetitive behaviour the person feels they have to do in response to these thoughts. OCD often begins in childhood, and, if left untreated, can cause significant problems as an adult.

Body dysmorphic disorder (BDD): Here, a child or young person worries excessively about things in their appearance that are either not noticeable to others, or only appear to be slight or insignificant to others. The most common body areas people with BDD worry about are facial features and skin appearance, but it can be about any part of the body. The person goes to great lengths to disguise these 'problems', for example, using excessive make-up or wearing particular clothes to hide the perceived problem. The most common age for BDD to start is around 12 or 13, and two thirds of people with BDD develop it before they are 18.

Other obsessional disorders that can start in childhood include hoarding, which is when people find it difficult to get rid of things they don't need and feel they must save. In children this can start with small piles of rubbish or collections of insignificant things. There is also trichotillomania, when a person pulls out their own hair, resulting in hair loss, and excoriation disorder, which involves compulsively picking at the skin.

We do not cover obsessional problems specifically in this book. Whilst your child might find some of the exercises helpful, if you believe your child might have an obsessional illness, please speak to your doctor and ask for a referral for treatment. It's worth remembering that one anxiety or obsessional problem can exist alongside others ('co-morbidity') so if you have one problem, you're quite likely to have others too. If this is the case, please don't worry; it is not at all uncommon and treatment still works. It would be best to speak to a professional to help with a treatment plan on which disorder to focus on first.

DEPRESSION ALONGSIDE ANXIETY

"It is estimated that 10-15 per cent of children with an anxiety problem may also be depressed."

Depression can occur alongside anxiety problems in children. It is estimated that 10-15 per cent of children with an anxiety problem may also be depressed. This makes sense because if you are excessively worried about something, it tends to follow that you will feel down and withdrawn. For example, if your child has anxiety around social situations, they may avoid social events and positive interpersonal interactions with peers, thus removing the chance for enjoyable activities. This would likely cause them to have a low mood.

However, the jury is still out on the causal relationship between childhood anxiety disorders and depression. Indeed, depression may be linked to a genetic predisposition, or it may be a result of symptoms overlapping between anxiety and depression. Depression occurs more in some anxiety problems, such as generalised anxiety disorder. Just because your child is anxious does not meant they are depressed, although it is worth considering.

"If depression has occurred because of an anxiety problem, it will likely improve when the anxiety problem resolves."

DEPRESSION SYMPTOMS IN CHILDREN

Depression is when a low mood lasts for more than two weeks, with symptoms including irritability, changes in appetite (including loss of appetite or increased eating), insomnia or excessive sleeping, reluctance to socialize, lack of energy and motivation, and increased tearfulness.

Depression in children is assessed on the same criteria as adults, but children may show different symptoms.

Children are more likely to present with somatic symptoms such as headaches, stomachaches, fatigue and pain, and instead of a flat mood, their mood might be up and down a lot. They might show anger, irritability and outbursts.

You may also see a lot of behaviour problems, disrupted sleep, weight loss and an increase in anxiety symptoms.

TIP

If you are worried that your child is suffering from depression, speak to a professional for more help and guidance.

While feeling low occasionally is normal, depression is a more serious and lengthy condition for young people because it can be harder for them to see the way through it. A proper assessment and diagnosis are important, and an evidence-based treatment approach can then be started.

If depression has occurred because of an anxiety problem, it will likely improve when the anxiety problem resolves, but it is still important to seek professional help if you think your child is depressed.

SUMMARY

This chapter has explained what worry and anxiety are, and when normal thoughts of worry and anxiety become a problem. We have also looked at the main symptoms for anxiety and common anxiety disorders.

We will now move on to how your child may experience anxiety, and how to discuss this with them.

CHAPTER 2

YOUR CHILD'S WORRIES AND ANXIETY

"Children may not always know what the 'bad thing' is that they are worried about. Instead, they experience a feeling of overwhelming dread that something bad will happen."

It may be clear to you after reading Chapter 1 that your child is struggling with worrying thoughts. However, children – especially younger ones – might have trouble saying exactly *what* it is that is making them anxious.

It is important to understand that children may not always *know* what the 'bad thing' or catastrophic outcome is that they are worried about. Instead, they experience a vague feeling of overwhelming dread that something bad will happen or is about to happen.

WHAT COULD YOUR CHILD WORRY ABOUT?

As covered in Chapter 1, anxiety is a very normal part of being human. Having worries is also normal in children. They worry about the same things that adults do, but in an age-appropriate way, such as social situations, school, friends, some form of harm happening to themselves or others, and not fitting in with peers etc.

Indeed, there are common areas in which a child's worry manifests, such as school life, friendships, family dynamics and life changes.

'NORMAL' FEARS AND WORRIES FOR CHILDREN

Children appear to develop fears according to what they can understand and the environment around them. Below is a broad look at what each age range could worry about.

Younger children
Fear of separation from primary caregivers.

6 year olds
Worries of loss of separation from caregivers.
Specific fears, like being scared of the dark or animals.

10-13 year olds
Worry about personal injury, death, natural disasters and danger.

13 year olds onwards
Social comparisons, anxiety about not performing well, failure and physical appearance.

While this book is focused on the 4–11 year old age range, you may recognize some of the older worries in your pre-teen.

HOW TO TALK ABOUT WORRY

When discussing worries with your child, it is essential to normalize worry and to reassure them that you can help them through it. It may be that your child won't want to open up to you immediately – this is fine, as some children take longer to process things and may want to speak later.

The most important thing you can do is to let them know that you are there to help them when they are ready to talk. You may wish to give them an example of when you have been worried and were able to work through it with someone. Here are some suggestions:

- *Everyone worries, even me! It can be good to share worries so we can work them out together.*
- *When I was your age, I worried about whether my schoolwork was good enough. When I spoke to my mother, she said that mistakes were normal and as long as I learned from them, it was fine to make them.*
- *When things bother us, it can be hard to make sense of them, so sharing them helps us to gain perspective and work through them together.*

- *Having problems or things you are not sure about is normal. You are just like everyone else.*

The questions in the activity opposite are leading questions and are a great way to open up important conversations about worry or anxiety. They are a device that can help your child put their worries and thoughts into words.

> "The most important thing you can do is to let them know that you are there to help your child when they are ready to talk about it."

If a relaxed, non-judgemental chat, with no expectations, happens every now and again, then worrying – and talking about worrying – can begin to be normalized.

TIP

A good way to have these conversations is to chat whilst doing another fun activity like a board game, jigsaw puzzle or even out on a bike ride.

Don't worry if your child doesn't want to talk about it then, don't persist and try again another day. It is enough that they know you care and are available to talk to them.

ACTIVITY:
Start Talking

One icebreaker is to start talking about how worrying feels and how worrying makes your child feel.

This is a good opener because even if children are unsure as to what worry is, they should easily be able to recognize the physical signs of it being present.

Explain to your child that when we worry, our bodies react in lots of different ways. We might notice:

- Tummy butterflies
- Jelly legs
- A dry mouth
- Breathlessness
- Stomachache
- Tingly feelings
- A fast heartbeat
- Shivering
- Dizziness
- Feeling sick

When you've gone through the list above, ask your child:

- *How do you feel when you are worried?*
- *Which bits of your body feels funny or different?*
- *Do you feel any of the things in the list?*
- *When do you get these feelings?*
- *How long do these feelings last for?*
- *How do you describe this feeling? E.g. hot, shaky, etc.*

It is good to use the terms that the child uses and feels comfortable with. For example, if Junaid says he feels like he has a shakey tummy and hot head, use these descriptions when speaking about worries: 'When was the last time you felt like you had a shakey tummy and hot head?'

RECOGNIZING ANXIETY IN YOUR CHILD

If you're having trouble getting your child to articulate what they are struggling with, don't worry. That your child is feeling anxious about *something* is enough for you to be able to help them. Even if you can't quite tell what it is, you can gather that they are responding to a situation that feels threatening. You don't always need to figure out what the problem is before starting to help.

"You don't always need to figure out what the problem is before starting to help."

In children, avoiding something is a key sign that there is a problem. Because they can't always say exactly what is worrying them, younger children make excuses to avoid the situation.

Headaches, stomachaches and feeling sick are very common symptoms of anxiety and if you've gone through the standard checks to make sure there is nothing physically wrong with your child (i.e. raised temperature, diarrhoea or vomiting), you can start to think about whether it is a response to a situation they find frightening and are worried about.

> "That your child is feeling anxious about *something* is enough for you to be able to help them – even if you can't quite tell what it is."

They might also say that they don't want to go to school or begin to ask repeated questions on the same topic to seek reassurance. Of course, this could pass very quickly without you having to do anything, but if it goes on for weeks, you are best to intervene to try to help your child understand and overcome the problem.

Return also to the list of symptoms on page 35 to recall which of these you felt your child experienced.

HOW YOUR CHILD'S ANXIETY COULD AFFECT THE FAMILY

A child's anxiety problem can affect all members of the family, often without it being obvious.

It may be that other children's needs or problems are ignored, or that the family stops doing certain activities because the child is worried about it.

One child's anxiety can cause stress, resentment and conflict within a family, but remember this is hopefully a phase and will get better when your child begins to recover.

It can be very helpful to sit down as a family and discuss the problem and the how it is affecting everyone.

Ask other family members to be patient and supportive while you all work together to try and help the individual.

If your child sees a professional, it may be a good idea to request a family session, too. This would help everyone to understand the problem and know how they can help the family member overcome it.

SUMMARY

Encouraging your child to talk about what is worrying them, and normalizing the conversation around anxiety and the physiological symptoms is a really powerful tool in helping your child.

Try and have regular conversations with your child about what might be bothering them. Do it in a relaxed, comfortable way.

If your child doesn't verbalize what's worrying them, you may notice symptoms of anxiety instead.

Consider the effects of your child's anxiety on the wider family.

You don't have to know how the anxiety problem started to start helping your child.

CHAPTER 3

YOUR CHILD'S THOUGHT PROCESS

"Worries are clever because they like to lead us into 'thinking traps', which means we get stuck in the unhelpful ways we think."

If you suffer with anxious thoughts yourself, you may have an idea about the kind of thinking processes your child may be experiencing. If you don't it can be hard to understand how they have come to think in this way.

This chapter will explain the thinking processes that can lead to overwhelming worry and anxious thoughts. You may recognize some traits of your own child.

First, let's consider if it's possible for your child to stop worrying altogether, and how people try (and fail) to do this.

CAN YOU GET RID OF WORRIES?

Is it possible to stop worrying? In your own life, you have probably been told – lots of times – to 'stop worrying' because your worries are 'all in your head'. You may have even told your child this. But the problem with worry is that it likes to stick around. And no matter how hard you try, it can be very hard to shake off a worrying thought, or sense that something is wrong. It hangs around like a black cloud over your head.

People try all sorts of ways to get rid of their worries:

- They might *block them out.* This can work well initially, but only for a short time as worries tend to return.
- They might *avoid people and places* (and even stop doing things they like doing) because they remind them of their worry.
- They seek reassurance that the worries will not happen.
- They might develop little habits that help them avoid the worries.
- Children might say special words, count in numbers or have 'lucky' things (clothes, toys and other objects) to help get rid of their worries (this is obsessive compulsive disorder, and whilst we don't cover it specifically, it can be helpful to understand anxiety first before treating the OCD).

"It can be very hard to shake off a worrying thought. It hangs around like a black cloud over your head."

Trying to avoid coming across worries, or trying to make them go away, is very normal. The problem is, that is not an effective solution. Unless worries are dealt with properly, they will keep returning.

YOUR CHILD'S THINKING TRAPS

Worries are clever because they like to lead us into 'thinking traps', which means we get stuck in the unhelpful ways we think. It can be very difficult to get out of the trap if you don't recognize it.

There are several different kinds of thinking traps common in anxiety. Consider whether you have heard your child echo any of these thinking processes. The activities in Part 2 will help you address these thinking traps and help your child reframe their worries, offering a different perspective and more positive thought pattern.

DISASTER THINKING

Quite often, we worry about things that might happen in the future, even though they may never happen. We also worry about things that have happened once (a thunderstorm, for example), but might not happen again for a while. We can think the worst is going to happen and that everything will be a disaster.

TIP

Help your child to realize that worrying disasters very rarely come true. Talk about volcanoes or avalanches – events that very rarely happen. They can seem more likely than they actually are. Worries are like this; they seem more likely to come true but, in fact, rarely do.

SNOWBALLING

If you roll a small snowball across a field of snow, it will grow bigger and bigger as it picks up more snow. Worries can be like snowballs. For example, imagine the scenario that your child is learning to ride a bike and they're worried about falling off. They worry about this because falling off might mean that they:

- Get hurt.
- See other kids laughing at them.
- Damage their bike.
- Are too scared to get back on.
- Worry about never learning to ride.
- Worry they'll be left out by friends.
- Worry that something is wrong with them.

See how the worry has snowballed from something small into a big thing?

TIP

Explain to your child that if the first worry comes true, it doesn't mean that the other worries will come true as well.

'GOOD' AND 'BAD' FEELINGS

This is when a person is only able to stop worrying when they feel 'good' emotions such as happiness or excitement and so they think they have to feel this way all of the time to not be anxious. Of course, we all spend a lot of time trying to feel 'good' emotions and do everything we can not to feel the 'bad' ones (if we feel angry, we try to be nice; if we feel sad, we try to look happy). However, 'bad feelings' are still normal feelings even if they are uncomfortable – and if you don't fight them and let them stay for a little while, they can be more easily dealt with.

"All feelings are normal and can be helpful guides."

There are, in fact, no such things as 'good' and 'bad' feelings. All feelings are normal and can be helpful guides. Anger allows us to consider other people's actions and ensure we are not taken advantage of; sadness is appropriate when certain events happen like loss; and frustration when things are not going right can help us learn to refocus and try again. Think about whether you have labelled feelings as 'bad' or 'not ok' or discouraged your child from expressing them. This might lead them to consider some feelings as 'bad' or 'not allowed' and can cause them to hide them or channel them in other less-constructive ways.

TIP

Encourage your child to allow their feelings of anger, sadness and other emotions that may have been labelled as 'bad' or 'unhelpful' to come out.

Normalize all feelings, and help your child work on ways to express that emotion. For example, jumping on the trampoline when feeling angry and then being able to talk about why they are feeling angry.

Remind your child that trying to feel 'good' emotions all of the time is exhausting, unsustainable and unrealistic. Normalize all emotions, even the unpleasant ones, and teach that they will pass.

FORTUNE TELLING

Sometimes we worry about the future because we think we can predict it. For example, a child might worry about their pet getting run over or something bad happening at school, but you can never know exactly what will happen in the future so remind your child that there is little point worrying about it.

TIP

Explain to your child that their future worry is something that hasn't happened yet and might never happen. And even if it does, worrying about it won't change it!

Try looking at all of the possibilities of an event, even the crazy ones. This will show that it's not possible to know exactly what an outcome will be so worrying about it too much isn't productive.

MAGICAL THINKING

This is when you do something to stop something bad from happening, such as counting, saying particular words or doing things in a strict pattern. For example, Jack's granny was in hospital and Jack thought that if he counted to ten every two hours, she wouldn't die. It's healthy and normal for Jack to be concerned about his granny, but counting to ten is adding an extra layer of intensity to his worries.

TIP

Talk with your child about how it is not possible to change things from happening by making a spell. Make some outlandish spells to prove that they don't work!

SUMMARY

It isn't possible to simply get rid of worries.

If your child uses avoidance or tries to find ways of coping with these thoughts, without addressing them, it might make the worries quieter for a bit, but it will not change them and they will return.

Your child may exhibit several different negative thinking traps, and helping them challenge these will help your child to see they are not realistic or helpful.

It is possible for your child to change the way they think, and you can help them do this by using some of the advice in this chapter, and in the next part of the book.

CHAPTER 4

ACCEPTING ANXIETY

*"Accepting anxiety and worry
as normal will help your
child's recovery."*

You may have recognized a fair few thought traps that your
child steps into in the previous chapter. And your immediate
reaction is probably to want to solve their problem, to do
whatever you can to eradicate all negative or troublesome
thoughts.

In this chapter, before we move on to the activities of Part 2, I
want to emphasise how and why we should *accept* anxiety and
worry as normal in order to help your child's recovery.

SUMMARIZING WORRY AND ANXIETY

Let's recap on some of the main points of Part 1 so far.

- Anxiety is a normal response to something we consider
  to be threatening.
- Anxiety is a primal response to threat, better known as
  'fight, flight or freeze'. It's a defence mechanism. We all
  need this response in our lives to keep us alive and safe.

- Anxiety becomes problematic when we interpret something as more threatening than it is, or we misinterpret a situation as threatening, when it is not.
- We all experience anxiety (and worry and fear) at times in our lives.
- Worries are thoughts, and 'anxiety' describes the emotions and bodily symptoms felt as a result of those worries/thoughts.
- Anxiety and worry occur for all sorts of reasons and are common. What makes it a problem is when it has a significant effect on our lives. It might prevent your child from doing things previously enjoyed, or make them want to avoid situations and people.
- When faced with worry and anxiety, we can learn to think differently and find different ways to challenge the anxiety.

THE IMPORTANCE OF NORMALIZING AND ACCEPTANCE

Working with your child to accept their anxiety is much better than fighting it. By accepting worries and anxieties for what they are, there is no need to run away from them. Instead, we approach them and deal with them, and learn to live life without being affected by them.

Acceptance of all emotions, including anxiety and fear, is important. Until all feelings are accepted, they will be considered a burden and will become problematic over time.

> "The goal is not to avoid or to get rid of difficult or unpleasant emotions; it is to accept them."

Remember that all thoughts, whether nice or uncomfortable, come from the same place in the brain. We so easily accept pleasant thoughts and the nice emotions associated with them, but we so rarely accept the thoughts that cause discomfort or distress.

TIP

One way to accept anxiety and worry is to normalize it. See the Normalize Worry activity on page 103.

So, the goal is not to avoid or to get rid of difficult or unpleasant emotions; it is to accept them, normalize them and ensure that they are not being experienced too frequently or intensely.

By working with your child to address worrying thoughts and stop giving them too much time and significance, they will hopefully start to come and go just as easily as 'good' thoughts. Part 2 is full of activities that will help you to do this.

SUMMARY

Acceptance is about accepting all emotions and thoughts, and not trying to block or avoid them.

By accepting anxiety and worry, we can actively deal with them in a positive and helpful way.

ANXIETY CHECKLIST

To end part 1, read through this checklist and see which apply to your child.

At this stage, it's not vital to 'nail down' exactly what the problem is, where it lies or how it affects them – just acknowledging that there is a problem is a good start.

- Does your child have any sleep problems (e.g. finding it hard to get to sleep, waking up in the night, feeling excessively tired in the morning)?
- Does your child often seem irritable, on edge or tearful?
- Does your child tend to be excessively clingy and seem unwilling to be parted from you or other loved ones, even for short periods?
- Does your child experience tearfulness/moodiness?
- Does your child try to avoid going to school?
- Has your child experienced changes in behaviour or started to avoid things they used to like?
- Is your child withdrawn or becoming isolated?
- Does your child worry excessively about terrible things happening?
- Does your child do anything to avoid having these worries?
- Does your child repeatedly ask for reassurance that things will be OK?
- Has your child voiced a number of worries or concerns either about a specific topic or about many things?

- Does your child seem caught up in their thoughts more than usual?

Through these questions, you should have built up a picture of how your child experiences anxiety, and identified some things your child worries about.

It can be a bit daunting to build up this picture, but know that you are now armed with the knowledge that can help you help your child.

The next step is talking to your child on a regular basis, and being creative in the ways you get them to open up about their thoughts.

PART 2

WHAT CAN YOU DO TO HELP YOUR CHILD?

CHAPTER 5

THE FOUR BUILDING BLOCKS FOR PARENTS

"This chapter will show you the best mindset to have, and approach to take, to help your child."

Now that we've explored how and why your child may be experiencing worry and anxiety, we'll turn our attention to what you can do about it.

The next chapter contains lots of activities to help challenge your child's worries and anxious thoughts. This chapter will show you the best mindset to have, and approach to take with your child, before starting the activities.

We will look at four 'building blocks' that can make a real difference to your child.

These are to:

1. Tackle problems in a positive way
2. Provide the right kind of support
3. Encourage self-kindness
4. Prioritize sleep

1. TACKLE PROBLEMS IN A POSITIVE WAY

When faced with a child who is very worried about something, it's quite easy as a parent to exacerbate the situation, to subconsciously feed into their worry with questions, body language or by trying to take the problem away so your child doesn't have to deal with it. This isn't the best thing for your child.

> "Positive reinforcement does not mean reassuring your child that 'everything will be alright', but should be an acknowledgement that your child has made an effort to face their fear."

Try and find ways of addressing the problem in a positive way – for example, if your child has had worries about going to school, but these have gone away, it is vital to follow that up with *positive reinforcement*. This is not reassurance that 'everything will be alright' (which is not always helpful, as we will see), but an acknowledgement that your child has made an effort to face their fear. Give a verbal reward by praising them, or physical rewards such as a treat, a cuddle, reading or playing a game with them, and be clear about which behaviour you are praising.

> **TIP**
> Rewards are a 'well done' for positive behaviour. They
> should be applied as soon as possible after the event. Don't
> leave them too late, otherwise they lose their power!

"When you acknowledge worries, you help to normalize them."

If a situation doesn't go well, and your child is really struggling to 'pull it together', remember to encourage, not punish or discourage.

Being *discouraging* is to respond unhelpfully to behaviours that you have identified as a problem.

For example, take the mother whose child was anxious about going to school and refused to get changed into his uniform. So, she put her child into the car and dropped him off in his pyjamas. This did nothing but reinforce her child's worries about school. Instead, the mother needed to tell her child that although he was worried, worries are normal and he was being brave by getting out of bed and putting on his school uniform. She then needed to reward him when he came home from school in some way.

"If we use negative reinforcement, it doesn't help children deal with the worries; it only makes them hide them and endure the worrying situation with a lot of distress."

When you acknowledge worries, you help to normalize them. Using negative reinforcement (i.e. punishment) amplifies anxieties in the same way that if you kick a dog when it doesn't retrieve a ball, you end up with a highly strung creature that only responds to you out of the fear of being punished, not because they want to play with you. So if we use negative reinforcement for children with their worries, it doesn't help them deal with the worries; it only makes children hide them and endure the worrying situation with a lot of distress.

2. PROVIDE THE RIGHT KIND OF REASSURANCE

It can be a knee-jerk reaction to want to tell your child with anxiety that 'everything will be alright'. But this reassurance is not the most helpful thing for your child.

This reassurance often reinforces their anxiety and 'enough reassurance' will never be enough. Seeking reassurance can become an unhelpful 'safety behaviour' itself.

SAFETY BEHAVIOURS

Safety behaviours are the behaviours we rely on when we have an anxiety problem because we believe that they will protect us from the feared consequence. They often include avoidance (when people try to avoid the thoughts, feelings and situations that frighten them in the hope it will keep them 'safe') or seeking reassurance from people about a particular worry or worrying situation.

That said, it is hard *not* to reassure someone that they will be okay, especially when it's your child in distress. However, if the reassurance is given incorrectly it can lead the child to feel more distressed and less trustful of what you are saying.

"Seeking reassurance can becomes an unhelpful 'safety behaviour' itself."

Take a look at the following examples, all of which show that reassurance might not the best thing to combat anxiety.

- If your child is worried about going to school because it is Book Week and they are anxious about having to talk about their favourite book, don't say, 'It will be fine, maybe you won't have to do it'. Instead, try saying, 'I understand it can be overwhelming talking in front of people, but that is normal and the more you do it, the easier it gets.'

- If your child is worried about starting a new class or trying a new leisure activity, don't say 'You'll be fine! Nothing to worry about.' Instead, say, 'You are so brave to be trying something new. We don't know how it will go, but I hope you enjoy it.' Encourage your child to be brave, letting them know that facing the situation is never as bad as imagined.

This isn't the easiest path to take, but if it is done with kindness and understanding, it is the best approach by far.

"Ask yourself, 'Am I doing anything to feed into this worry, allowing it to grow, or telling my child the feared event won't happen?'"

Family members can unwittingly collude in anxiety by reassuring or allowing the child to avoid certain situations like going to school. If this is you, you need to ask yourself, 'Am I doing anything to feed into this worry, allowing it to grow, or telling my child the feared event won't happen?' If so, you need to stop doing this and find other ways to help them. This might be harder in the short term as it will mean your child has to face their fears and deal with the anxiety, but in the longer term it prevents the anxiety problem from growing bigger and teaches your child to face their fears when they have them.

3. ENCOURAGE SELF-KINDNESS

To overcome an anxiety problem, one of the best things you can teach your child is how to build self-kindness.

By highlighting the importance of being kind to yourself, you can explain that anxiety makes it very easy to be self-critical. It is easy to feel ashamed and embarrassed about having worry problems, but these kinds of feelings can hold your child back from getting better.

> "Encourage your child to be kind to themselves. This will help them accept their thoughts – and themselves."

Encourage your child to be kind to themselves, and to not berate themselves if they worry when they are really trying not to. This will help them accept their thoughts – and themselves. It might help to show them that others struggle with anxiety too, so they don't feel so alone. See the Normalize Worry activity on page 103.

TIP

Tell your child: 'Never forget – you are a wonderful, worthwhile person. You deserve to be supported and treated with kindness.'

---

4. PRIORITIZE SLEEP

"Sleep can help make any worry problem feel more manageable."

Sleep is very important. If you have a good night's sleep, you feel great. It's good for body and mind, and can help make any worry problem feel more manageable. Not getting enough sleep can affect your child's schoolwork, and it can also make them feel sad and depressed. You need to be extra careful if anxiety is an issue because it will only get worse the more tired the person feels, so please be mindful of this.

Children need a lot of sleep. Probably more than you think! Three- to six-year-olds need between ten and 12 hours per night; seven- to 12-year-olds need ten to 11 hours.

If your child finds it hard to get to sleep, try the below tips.

BEFORE BED
Eat Right

Cut down on sugary, fizzy drinks. Lots of them contain caffeine, which keeps people awake. If your child likes a night-time drink before bed, give them a nice mug of warm milk. Also, don't allow too many sugary snacks, especially later in the day. You don't want your child to be full of sugar and buzzing with energy just before bedtime!

Exercise Enough

Children who get plenty of exercise in the day sleep better at night. And even better, exercise beats stress – so it's a great way to tackle anxiety.

Limit Screen Time

A bit of TV or screen time is fine, just not too much and not straight before bed. Remember, kids are also accessing screens at school for learning these days, too. Encourage them not to use a screen for an hour or so before bed.

Debrief Before Bed

Get the worries out before bedtime. Help your child to write down the worries that are swirling around in their head and assure them you can work through this list together tomorrow. This is better done a couple of hours before bed ideally, so they are not overthinking worries.

BEDTIME

The activities in this book should be completed at an earlier time in the day – not right before bed. This makes sure when your child is getting in a state ready for bed they don't become too 'wired' or upset. Below are some tips to create optimum sleeping conditions.

Routine is Key

A set bedtime routine can help prepare the body for sleep. Include a relaxing bath time, stories and a chat before bed, and it could become a really special part of the day.

Bath Before Bed

Having a shower or bath before bed can help the body prepare for sleep by raising the body temperature and relaxing it.

Monitor the Light

Try not to have too much light in the room. As it gets darker, our bodies start to get ready for sleep. A little night light is perfectly fine.

Temperature Check

Get the room temperature right, because having a room that is too cold or too hot can make it difficult to sleep.

It is recommended that 18 degrees Celsius (64.4 degrees Fahrenheit) is the best temperature for sleeping at night.

Soothing Sounds

Some people like to listen to calming sounds when they go to bed. Is this something your child would like? Perhaps waves on a beach or some classical music or white noise?

"Help your child to write down the worries
that are swirling around in their head and
assure them you can work through this list
together tomorrow."

TIP

If you are putting your child to sleep, and they start
mentioning worries, try and write them down on a piece
of paper, put them in a jar and tell your child you will work
through these tomorrow. This can help them feel listened
to and that they have gotten the worries out of their head.

Make sure not to worry if the bedtime advice opposite doesn't
always work and your child still struggles to get to sleep. Just
like adults, children experience nights when they can't drop
off to sleep. You might need to play around with your own
routines a bit until you find what works for you and your family.

SUMMARY

"Show that you understand but do not try
and vanish the problem with reassurance."

Be sure to bear these four building blocks in mind when you move
on to the next chapter, where we look at some activities you can
do with your child to help them with their worries and anxiety.

When you are doing each activity, remember to:

- Always be positive, and encouraging.
- Show that you understand but do not try and vanish the problem with reassurance.
- Encourage your child be kind to themselves.
- Make sure your child has a calm bedtime and the opportunity to get enough sleep.

CHAPTER 6

ACTIVITIES TO CHANGE YOUR CHILD'S THOUGHT PROCESS

"These activities can be helpful if you notice your child entering into a thinking trap, to change their thoughts into something positive or offer a different perspective."

In this chapter, we will look at a variety of ways to encourage your child to challenge their thought processes, and invite more positive thoughts into their mind. There are a lot of activities in this chapter – take your time to try these with your child. Some may work better than others, but hopefully some of them may lead to a good conversation about their thoughts and feelings.

All of these activities will help to challenge your child's thinking traps (see page 61), and can be helpful if you notice your child entering into a thinking trap, to change their thoughts into something positive or offer a different perspective.

"Hopefully the activities will lead to a good conversation about your child's thoughts and feelings."

"Worries will start to feel
smaller and more manageable
when they are addressed and
talked about."

If you and your child do one of these activities a few times a week, it's amazing how quickly results can appear. Worries will start to feel smaller and more manageable when they are addressed and talked about.

TIP

All the activities included can be used for any aged child, with a little adaptation.

However, some activities are especially good for younger children (4–7 year olds), while others work well with older children in our age range (8–11 year olds).

We have noted this in the activity introduction.

WORRIES WILL PASS

> "The Worry Bus helps children see that worries are just thoughts and do not need to stick around in their heads."

Worries can often seem big and overwhelming, and constantly there, but they don't need to be.

The Worry Bus activity below helps your child recognize any worries they have and learn a way to manage them. The Worry Bus does this by helping them see that worries are just thoughts and do not need to stick around in their heads.

This activity works really well with younger children who can get 'on board' with the role play.

ACTIVITY:
The Worry Bus

Imagine a Worry Bus. (You might need to explain that it's not a real bus, so you need to imagine it!)

What does it look like? What colour is it? Is it a single or double-decker?

Tell your child that they are the driver of the Worry Bus. How exciting! Or Mum or Dad can drive it. Whatever they prefer.

Tell your child:

- *The Worry Bus is magical because it picks up your worry and keeps it on the bus for a few minutes while it tries to talk to you.*
- *You are too busy driving the bus to notice what it is saying, but it is allowed to ride the bus just like anyone else.*
- *A worry might start off big, or it might be small and very chatty.*
- *When you reach the next stop, take a big breath and say goodbye to it and tell the worry it needs to get off.*
- *Some worries might stay for few more stops, but they'll get off eventually.*

Extend the activity by getting your child to draw the bus and the worries on it, and to give them funny faces and characters. Your child can wave at the worries as they get off the bus.

They might also like to draw new passengers who are positive, as an antidote to the worry. They could start to crowd the bus so no more worries can get on!

PUT WORRIES INTO PERSPECTIVE

An activity that can help put your child's worries into perspective is to put them in the context of the future.

Remind your child that the worry they're going through now, which seems so huge and vast, won't last forever.

This is especially useful for older children who can both grasp the concept of the future and understand the transient nature of life.

> "Remind your child that the worry they're going through now, which seems so huge and vast, won't last forever."

This is still a good activity to do with younger children – they may not understand the concept of the future, or time in general, but talking with them about how the mind changes over time can still be effective. Younger children can work within a smaller time frame – perhaps in days or seasons.

ACTIVITY:
In One or Two Years' Time...

Discuss with your child one thing that is particularly worrying them at the moment. It can be anything.

Now, ask your child if they think that worry will still be obvious in a year. One year is a long time for children!

For example, you might say to an eight year old, 'When you are nine or 10 years old... That's two whole Christmases away.' Chances are that it won't seem so worrying anymore.

Discuss with your child that worries come and go and something that seems terrifying today may not seem that way even tomorrow, or next week.

Remind them of things they worried about in the past which did not come true, or that they don't worry about now.

For example, when they were a toddler they worried about the loud noises from trucks driving past; that doesn't worry them now.

Or last year they worried about Book Week costumes, but now they are excited about dressing up as a pirate!

FOCUS ON NICE MEMORIES

Worry can feel overwhelming and all-encompassing, and it can be hard for your child to remember that they didn't always feel this way. This activity helps them remember a time when they felt free of their anxious thoughts. This works well with any aged child.

ACTIVITY:
Good Memories

1. Get your child to think of a recent fun memory or a story from the past. Ask them to describe what happened, and their favourite part.
2. Get them to draw or write down what happened.
3. Get them to remember the details – the weather, the time of day, who was with them, how they got there, etc. This is because all the details will help bring up the positive emotions associated with the memory and make it feel more real.
4. You may need to prompt them occasionally, or use a photo or something else to remind them (a postcard, or their favourite snack they ate when they were there).
5. Remind them that those times were positive and they had fun, despite feeling worried sometimes.

If this went well, ask your child to think about future events they are looking forward to, as this will show them that despite feeling worried, they can still enjoy things and get excited about them.

IMAGINE POSITIVE ENDINGS

Instead of thinking about bad things that might happen, encourage your child to think about positive things that have happened or may happen instead. They can create a new story about what they are worrying about – one that makes them feel happy and excited, instead of nervous or worried. It's surprisingly possible to change the ending of a 'worry story' and make it different to the one their worry wants them to believe.

This activity will help your child to create a new story and a new ending. It will also teach them that even if you expect something bad to happen because you've worried about it, the narrative can go differently. It's also quite fun to make up different endings with you child!

ACTIVITY:
Switching the Story

Worries can be treated like a story and this narrative can be controlled. A worry can make you think only about bad outcomes, but if you try to create a new story or ending and visualize this happening, it can help your child to cope with their thoughts and, ultimately, make a more positive version of them.

Follow the below steps:

- Get your child to think about a worry.
- Ask them about their expectations of what might happen. What's the ending?
- Draw or write out this version of the story.
- Then, discuss an alternative ending, which ends positively.
- Draw or write out one or two more different endings to the story.
- Discuss how all options are likely and are potential outcomes to their worry, so why not choose a positive version to focus on?

For example:

Story: I'm worried about using roller skates for the first time.

The Worry Outcome: I'm going to fall off and scrape my knee, and I'll be scared to use them again. It's going to take a long time to use my skates well and there'll be lots of falling off.

Another Outcome: I'm going to try my hardest with learning to skate. I might fall but soon I will be whizzing around the streets. I can meet lots of new friends who also enjoy rollerskating.

"Even if you expect something bad to happen, the narrative can go differently."

FOCUS ON THE GOOD THINGS

A nice way to explain worry to your child and the importance of thinking positive things is to tell them to imagine their worries as weeds or flowers in a garden. If we feed the worries and give them a lot of attention (and water), they will grow bigger and crowd out the flowers growing.

However, if we cut them back and, instead, give the flowers the attention and care they need, then the flowers will blossom. Flowers are positive thoughts, and good things in life; if we focus on these, then they will flourish and bloom in our mind garden.

ACTIVITY:
Worries as Weeds or Flowers

1. Get your child to draw a garden, or collect weeds and flowers from outside and glue them to a piece of paper or card.
2. Explain that all gardens have weeds growing (the worries) – and that's ok – but the garden can still grow and flourish new flowers even if there are a few weeds.
3. The trick is to nourish the positive thoughts (flowers) and sow seeds for positive new thoughts.
4. Come up with some positive thoughts together and write them onto some colourful hand-drawn flowers or paste some fresh flowers over them.

NORMALIZE WORRY

Everyone has worries – old and young. The older we get, the more aware that we are about our own worries.

Normalize this with your child by getting them to name other people they know, grown-ups and children, and discuss what their worries may be. Then try to do some problem solving – coming up with simple solutions.

> "Everyone has worries – old and young. Normalize this by getting your child to name other people they know, and discuss what their worries may be."

If the problems are future based, then problem solving them *now* won't work. And again, emphasise that you cannot predict the future, but the trick is to do your best now and learn from the outcome (and that it is not as bad as feared). This is called resilience building.

This activity works well with older children, who may have the emotional intelligence and vocabulary to sense and articulate when others are feeling worried.

ACTIVITY:
Everyone Has Worries

1. Ask your child to draw a picture of people, each with a worry.
2. Make some of them trivial and some more serious. E.g. Grandma worries that the caterpillars will eat her lettuces and Charlie worries that no one at school will play with him.
3. Then, problem-solve each worry together – some won't take a long time to solve, but others might be tricker and require lots of thinking time and conversation. Some of them might not be able to be solved!
4. Normalize this. For example, Grandma might not be able to stop the caterpillars from eating all her lettuces this year, but she learns that the best thing to do next time is to cover them with some netting.
5. The key to problem-solving is making the worry seem more manageable. To do so, you can either focus on the content of the worry, or the consequences of the worry, and then come up with two or three problem-solving steps or resilience-building steps.

For example, with the problem of Charlie worrying that no one will play with him, here are some solutions:

1. He could ask someone to play or to join in a game with him.
2. He could speak to his older buddy at school who can check in with him at lunchtime.
3. His parent or caregiver could speak to his teacher before school so they are aware of his worry.
4. And if no one plays with him, he might decide to go to the library to read or to practise balancing on the playground beams.

At the end of the activity, show your child how you managed to solve all these different problems together, and you can do the same for their worries. Ask them if they want to do this now with you.

"This activity works well with older children, who may have the emotional intelligence and vocabulary to sense and articulate when others are feeling worried."

PRAISE BRAVERY

Even though your child might not know it, bravery is already within them. When they have overcome something that they worried about, they will build on this bravery. We learn from situations that make us nervous or worried, and we become braver by getting through them. Your child may just need this pointing out to them so they realize it. This activity is great for any aged child.

ACTIVITY:
What You've Already Achieved

Have a think together about all the brave things your child has already achieved, without realizing it. Here are some suggestions:

- Completing a first day at school.
- Going to the doctor for an injection.
- Going to the dentist.
- Travelling on an aeroplane.
- Performing on stage.
- Playing a big game of sport.

Discuss the examples and how your child felt before and after the event. Remind them that although it's not always easy being brave, if they keep practising, it will get easier each time. Then focus on the positive outcomes – that they really enjoyed the game or the performance, and they felt better after seeing the doctor.

A fun way of helping your younger child to feel brave is to talk to them about what kind of superhero they would like to be.

ACTIVITY:
Super Me!

Ask your child: What would their superhero name be? What would their outfit look like? What's their superpower? What would their trusty side-kick look like, and who would it be?

Ask them to have a think about what feelings that this character helps them to feel – brave? Invincible? Strong? Fierce? All of these?

Ask your child to close their eyes to 'lock in' all of these feelings.

Get your child to draw or make this superhero out of craft or Lego.

They might want to develop this character further – draw or build their hideout, and that they eat spinach and chips to feel brave, and have a monkey sidekick to remind them of their superhero powers.

Going forward, encourage your child to conjure up this character whenever they need a bravery boost.

TRY AND TRY AGAIN

Like a scientist, your child could try experimenting with worry and how to deal with it, and test out new ways of thinking to see what happens. This can help them challenge some of their anxious thoughts and change the way they think about them.

ACTIVITY:
Be a Scientist:

Follow the script below with your child:

Science is about understanding how our planet and people work, and scientists do lots of fun experiments to find out new things and learn new information.

But if an experiment doesn't go right, or how the scientist expected, the scientist doesn't give up.

Instead, they keep doing the experiment, until they get some answers.

They use the outcome to understand what happened, and what they expect to happen in the future.

With experiments it is important to:

- *Set up what theory the experiment is testing.*

- *Decide what you think the outcome will be.*
- *Record what the outcome actually is.*
- *Think what you can do next time to build on this.*

For example, Georgina was worried everyone at school would laugh at her after she had to start wearing glasses at school.

The experiment was: To test out other students' reactions to her glasses.

- *The theory she was testing was that everyone would laugh when they saw her glasses.*
- *She thought the outcome would be that everyone would look, stare and say horrible things.*
- *What actually happened was that a few kids made some comments, or asked her why she needed glasses, but mostly no one seemed to notice or care.*
- *Next time, she decided she might speak up in class more and not hide away so much, and see what the other students say.*

Let's think of some experiments we could do together.

Remember scientists do experiments repeatedly, so even if it goes well, or if you don't get the outcome expected, keep doing the experiment to see what happens. The more data you collect, the more confident you can be in your results.

CLIMB THE WORRY LADDER

A worry ladder is a great way for your child to start to make steps toward facing their worry. When they express that they have a worry, sit down with them and talk through the below by reading out the script (in your own words) and then doing the activity together.

> "A worry ladder is a great way for your child to start to make steps toward facing their worry."

You could try sketching some ladders with your child to illustrate the point and to help them imagine how their worry ladder might look. This works for any aged child – and even with grown ups!

ACTIVITY:
Taking Steps

Follow the script below with your child:

Imagine a ladder, how it goes higher and higher, and has plenty of steps.

Think about your worry. If you want to feel better about your worry, you need to climb up the ladder, one step at a time. Each rung of the ladder is a step closer to feeling brave about your worry.

Now, think of something that will place you on the first step of your worry ladder.

It might be giving a dog a stroke if you don't feel brave around them or signing up for the school play if you're nervous of being on stage. You might feel funny doing it, but I promise that once you do, it will feel amazing.

Set yourself some targets for each step and then make them bigger as you move up the ladder.

For example, if you're nervous about putting your hand up in class, set yourself a target of putting your hand up once on Monday, then you can do it twice the next day. And the day after that you can do it as many times as you want.

Celebrate each time you achieve something and climb further up the ladder! Soon, you'll reach the very top.

How do you feel? You have been so brave – well done!

ENCOURAGE DIFFERENT PERSPECTIVES

This activity helps children understand that there is more than one way to see a situation – particularly if there is something bothering them, or they are worried about something that happened.

It helps them to depersonalize some of the concerns they might have about what other people think about them.

This exercise works well with any aged child, and engages their imagination.

ACTIVITY:
We All Think Differently

Discuss a situation with your child, such as someone being upset on the bus or in the playground, and help them to come up with a thought for the other passengers or people playing in the playground.

For example: A little girl is crying at the playground.

Child 1: She must have hurt herself!

Child 2: She has lost her mother.

Bee 1: That is a loud flower!

Bee 2: That girl is scaring away the other bees, so I can have the flowers to myself. Great!

Parent 1: She's hungry and I can't find her snacks.

Parent 2: She's tired after a long day at school.

Dog: She is being too loud, so I can't focus on burying my bone.

You can have a lot of fun with this, thinking of all the different people and animals that might be considering the same situation completely differently.

Now, think of one of your child's worries and do the same exercise: get them to think about this worry from different perspectives, and show how it's possible to think differently about the same issue.

"You can have a lot of fun with this activity, thinking of all the different people and animals that might be considering the same situation completely differently."

SUMMARY

Hopefully some of these activities helped your child think about their anxious thoughts in a different way. The activities may have also encouraged your child to open up about their worries and anxious thoughts, which is great.

Make a note of the activities that your child particularly responded to so that you can revisit them.

If you manage to do one activity every few days, you will start seeing a gradual shift in your child's mindset quicker than you might think.

CHAPTER 7

IN THE MOMENT – WHEN YOUR CHILD IS ANXIOUS

"This is the chapter to turn to if your child seems to be in a spiral of worry and you're not sure how to get them out of it."

This chapter is full of different activities for you and your child to do together at times when your child is feeling particularly worried or anxious. They are in-the-moment activities that aim to calm your child, or distract them from their thoughts.

This is the chapter to turn to if your child seems to be in a spiral of worry and you're not sure how to get them out of it.

You might find some work better than others for your child – you know your child best, so please adapt them as you see fit. Make sure to begin each activity calmly, and your child will follow.

All of these activities work with any aged child, with some adaptation for age.

GET ON WITH THINGS

Telling worries to 'go away' doesn't work, at least not long-term. For those worries that hang around, explain to your child that they are there and might stay for a short time, but it's okay to get on with things despite the worry in the background. You never know; it could get bored being there without anything to do.

> "Explain to your child that worries might stay for a short time, but it's okay to get on with things despite the worry in the background."

This exercise is quick and calming, and a lovely thing to do together.

It can be done anywhere and anytime – it's portable! Do it in the park, before school in the playground, or at home before bedtime.

It might feel a bit funny to do at first, especially out and about, but with more practice, it will feel easier.

ACTIVITY:
Shrink the Worry

Find a comfortable place to be with your child – it might be their bedroom, where they can be surrounded by their favourite toys, books and pictures.

Together, close your eyes for a moment and think about the issue your child is worrying about. Follow the script below.

- *Let's try and shrink the worry in your mind. You can put in a very small box, or on top of a pin head, or let a caterpillar crawl away with it on its back.*
- *Imagine standing over your worries and feeling calm about them.*
- *Breathe slowly and feel a warmth spread through your body.*
- *Notice the sounds. Notice that things carry on.*

After a while, open your eyes and ask how your child feels. Did they notice their worry? Did it seem more manageable?

RELAX WITH AN ACTIVITY

Relaxation is important for everyone, but especially for anyone with worries.

When we worry, our bodies feel tense and nervous. That's because we are on alert for 'danger' – just like the cavemen deciding between whether to fight, take flight or freeze.

So, it's crucial that we find things to do that loosen our bodies and help us feel calm again. The same is very much true for children.

ACTIVITY:
Learning to Relax

Ask your child what they like to do to feel relaxed. Maybe they like colouring, drawing or writing; petting the dog; watching their favourite TV programme; cooking or playing football in the park. It might be tasks done alone or tasks with friends: building blocks, making a train set, doing a sticker book. It could be reading with a parent, or playing a card or board game.

There are lots of ways to relax – and just doing something that they enjoy probably means that they are relaxing! It's all about settling the body and the mind, and forgetting worry for a while.

DISTRACT WITH AN ACTIVITY

"This is not an avoidance technique – but will help children realize that the anxiety in their bodies will pass and the worry will become less important."

Distraction works very well when feeling anxious. Remember it's not about trying to shut the anxious thoughts away or get rid of them – this is not an avoidance technique – but this activity will help children realize that the anxiety in their bodies will pass and the worry will become less important. Distraction can also lead to new, positive thoughts – and fun!

ACTIVITY:
Distraction!

Help your child build up a list of possible activities to do when they are feeling physically overwhelmed by worry.

Often physical activity can be very helpful as it allows the body to work through the adrenaline and cortisol (stress hormones) that the body produces.

Don't make the task too demanding cognitively. It should be easy to do and fun. You can make these age-appropriate too.

Some examples include:

- Jumping on the trampoline.
- Using a skipping rope for five minutes.
- Going on a bike ride or scooter ride.
- Playing hide-and-seek with toys.
- Baking or making a snack.
- Making bubbles in the sink with soap.
- Having a bubble bath.
- Blowing bubbles.
- Dancing by copying a video.
- 10 minutes of yoga.
- Bouncing a ball.

Once you and your child have made the list, stick it somewhere prominent so that you can both refer to it when your child is needing distraction.

Get them to pick whatever they fancy and see how they feel after.

FIND A CALM PLACE

"Explain that this is a fun game all about staying still for a little while."

As well as relaxing with an activity, there are ways to relax without having to do anything at all!

This might appeal to your child or it might not, but it's worth having a go. There are also many apps for promoting relaxation, so it might be worth looking into these, too.

ACTIVITY:
Chill Time!

Try talking through the below script with your child, explaining that it's a fun game all about being calm and staying still for a little while.

Lie or sit down in a comfortable position in a quiet room.

When you have settled, tense the muscles in your feet, legs, arms, hands and face.

If you haven't done this before, imagine you're screwing them up tight. When they all feel 'tight', relax each part of your body, bit by bit.

Start with your feet, right down to your little toes.

Then your legs, both left and right.

Now point to your tummy – can you find it? Well done! And let it relax.

And the same with your chest.

Now wriggle your fingers, all ten of them, and let them go soft.

And let your arms flop by your side.

Finally, do a small smile and hold.

GET MOVING

"The more we exercise, the more our brain sends out signals to our body that we can be excited and active, rather than stressed and worried."

Worry can be beaten by being active. People who exercise regularly find that it stops them from feeling stressed and worried, because exercise sends positive chemicals from the brain to the body.

The more we exercise, the more our brain sends out signals to our body that we can be excited and active, rather than stressed and worried – and at the same time we become fitter and stronger, too.

This works as well for children as it does adults, and it's something that you can do together.

The obvious activity here is to go and do some exercise – a walk, a bike ride, a dance party. You might also want to try the activity opposite, as it encourages your child to think about what exercise inspires them – and then they're more likely to want to do it!

ACTIVITY:
Quick Questions

To promote thinking about (and doing!) physical activity, ask your child:

- *What is your favourite physical activity?*
- *Why is this?*
- *How often do you make time for it?*
- *How can you do this more often?*
- *Do you prefer team or solo games?*

Next, make a rough week plan together and work out where your child's favourite activity should fit into the week.

This will help to encourage and relax you, and to find room for their favourite exercise.

"Exercise works just as well for children as it does adults to reduce stress, and it's something that you can do together."

SUMMARY

At times when your child is really struggling with anxious thoughts, it's really tempting to tell them it's all going to be ok – and reassure them in the *wrong* way.

Next time your child is consumed by worry, try one of the activities in this chapter and notice the results.

Remember to make space for your child to talk to you about their worries, as well as trying these activities.

CHAPTER 8

MAKING PROGRESS

"My approach will help to create mental health skills that will help overcome worry and anxiety, so that your child can have a happier, healthier and more successful future."

I hope that this book has helped you help your child, by changing the impact of anxiety and worry for your child. I know how difficult it is to start on this journey; how challenging it can be to apply this approach to your family's situation.

But I also know that to do this successfully can bring untold rewards, bringing a life that is not dictated by anxiety and worry, and which has the stepping stones for a healthier mind.

"The aim is for your child to enjoy their life despite anxiety and worry, and to feel confident about new experiences and challenges."

A lot of the strategies we have discussed are useful as general tips for building resilience and happiness, too. The aim is for your child to enjoy their life despite anxiety and worry, and to feel confident about new experiences and challenges.

My approach is one that will help to create mental health skills that will help overcome worry and anxiety, so that your child can have a happier, healthier and more successful future.

SIGNS THAT YOUR CHILD HAS TURNED A CORNER

"By teaching your child the tools to understand and manage their worries, they are not ever back at 'step one', but will need encouragement to apply the strategies to new situations."

The path to managing anxiety will have its ups and downs. It is not one clear progress line, rather one with peaks and troughs. This is normal and expected, because life is up and down and constantly throws challenges at us. It may be that your child is doing well, then something happens that upsets them and they start worrying again. This is a setback, not a failure. By teaching your child the tools to understand and manage their worries, they are not ever back at 'step one', but will need encouragement to apply the strategies to new situations.

You may start seeing your child seem brighter in mood, and more positive about going to school. They might be upset less often, or upset about different things than the specific worry they had. They may feel brave enough to try new experiments and ways to tackle their worries, or they may even just stop talking about them. You might notice subtle signs in their behaviour that only you as a parent would notice. You know your child best, so you will know if they are making small improvements.

CELEBRATE SUCCESS

When your child begins to show signs of beating their anxiety or worry, or accepting them and being at peace with them, it will feel brilliant for you both. Be sure to celebrate this and to make a big deal of it. It's a huge and important step for everyone involved and wholly positive. It is useful to have a set of rewards in place so you can immediately reward them for their bravery.

"It is most important to reward your child for *trying* to overcome their worries, rather than the *actual* outcome."

It is most important to reward your child for *trying* to overcome their worries, rather than the *actual* outcome. The bravery and willingness to try will be what helps them overcome their worries the most.

IDEAS FOR REWARDS

- A special movie night.
- Doing one of their favoured activities with a parent.
- A new reading book or sticker book.
- An outing to somewhere special.
- Making (and eating) some celebratory cookies or muffins.
- A favourite family meal.

Now, think of some of your own ideas which will work well with your child.

WHAT IF ANXIOUS THOUGHTS COME BACK?

"Worry and anxiety may rear their head again, but your child will be able to use the strategies that they have learnt in the future."

The first thing to recognize is that you can't guarantee that your child's worries won't come back. There are no guarantees in life. Worry and anxiety may rear their head at different stages – for example, they may worry about performance at sport and school, or how they look, and so on. However, if they learn the skills to manage worries, they should be a good position to manage future worries in a similar way. They will build resilience and confidence, and be able to use these strategies going forward.

WAYS TO CONTINUE TO MANAGE WORRY

- Regularly try the exercises and techniques in this book with your child.
- Encourage your child to talk to you about it. Keep the conversation ongoing.
- Be understanding, but don't give in to the worries or be reassuring. For example, don't allow your child to stay home from school if they are worried about a presentation. Encourage them to do it but empathize with their worry.
- Talk to your child about what advice you both would give to someone else with worries, and try to take it on board.
- Lifestyle choices can affect your child's wellbeing – encourage them to exercise, sleep well and eat healthy food. Building a healthy body builds a healthy mind, and this will help to protect them from worry.

> "Your child will build resilience and confidence, and be able to use these strategies going forward."

FINAL NOTE

As a parent and a psychologist, I am very aware that all children suffer from anxiety at some point in their development, and that some children suffer more acutely than others. As a parent, you want to know the best way to help your child, but it can be difficult wading through all the information.

The strategies and advice in this book are based on Cognitive Behaviour Therapy (CBT) and are proven strategies in helping your child overcome anxiety and worry. Try the strategies and you may find that some of them work for your child better than others, and these are the ones they should practice.

> "By investing in your child's mental health and wellbeing, you are giving them the tools for a happier future."

Please be patient with yourself and your child. As the saying goes 'Good things take time' and it holds true here, too. Your child might not show improvements immediately, but they will hopefully do so over the weeks that you are working with them.

Stay calm and positive, especially if there is a setback or days when it seems like they have not made any progress. This is part of the journey and all journeys have their challenges. By investing in your child's mental health and wellbeing, you are giving them the tools for a happier future. You never know; you may learn something for yourself at the same time!

Please note if you are concerned about your child and they have made some progress with these steps, you might want to consider a formal diagnosis and individual CBT with a suitably trained professional.

I wish you all the best on your journey to better mental health for you and your family.

USEFUL RESOURCES

GENERAL MENTAL HEALTH RESOURCES
Many of these organizations have specific information on how to help children with their mental health.

UK
- Mental Health Foundation UK: www.mentalhealth.org.uk
- Mind UK: www.mind.org.uk
- Rethink Mental Illness: www.rethink.org
- Samaritans: www.samaritans.org, helpline: 116 123
- Scottish Association for Mental Health (SAMH) (Scotland): www.samh.org.uk
- Shout: www.giveusashout.org, text 85258

Europe
- Mental Health Europe: www.mhe-sme.org
- Mental Health Ireland: www.mentalhealthireland.ie

USA
- HelpGuide: www.helpguide.org
- Mentalhealth.gov: www.mentalhealth.gov
- Mental Health America: www.mhanational.org

- National Alliance on Mental Illness (NAMI): www.nami.org
- National Institute of Mental Health: www.nimh.nih.gov
- Very Well Mind: www.verywellmind.com

Canada
- Canadian Mental Health Association: cmha.ca
- Crisis Service Canada: www.ementalhealth.ca

Australia and New Zealand
- Beyond Blue: www.beyondblue.org.au
- Head to Health: headtohealth.gov.au
- Health Direct: www.healthdirect.gov.au
- Mental Health Australia: mhaustralia.org
- Mental Health Foundation of New Zealand: www.mentalhealth.org.nz
- SANE Australia: www.sane.org

CHILDREN'S MENTAL HEALTH RESOURCES
UK

- CHUMS (Mental Health and Emotional Wellbeing Service for Children and Young People): chums.uk.com
- NHS information: www.nhs.uk/oneyou/every-mind-matters/childrens-mental-health
- NSPCC: www.nspcc.org.uk
- Place2Be: www.place2be.org.uk
- Young Minds: www.youngminds.org.uk

Europe

- The Alliance for Childhood European Network Group: www.allianceforchildhood.eu
- ChildHub: childhub.org

USA

- Child Mind Institute: childmind.org
- Children's Mental Health Network: www.cmhnetwork.org
- Very Well Family: www.verywellfamily.com

Canada

- Caring for Kids: www.caringforkids.cps.ca

Australia and New Zealand

- Beyond Blue Health Families: healthyfamilies. beyondblue.org.au
- Kids Helpline (for young people aged between 5–25 years): www.kidshelpline.com.au
- ReachOut: www.about.au.reachout.com

ANXIETY-SPECIFIC RESOURCES

In the following websites you can find guidance, support, advice and treatment options.

UK

- Anxiety UK: www.anxietyuk.org.uk, helpline: 03444 775 774
- No More Panic: www.nomorepanic.co.uk
- No panic: www.nopanic.org.uk
- Social Anxiety: www.social-anxiety.org.uk

USA

- Anxiety and Depression Association of America: www.adaa.org

Canada

- Anxiety Canada: www.anxietycanada.com

Australia and New Zealand

- Anxiety New Zealand Trust: www.anxiety.org.nz
- Black Dog Institute: www.blackdoginstitute.org.au

ABOUT US

Welbeck Balance publishes books dedicated to changing lives. Our mission is to deliver life enhancing books to help improve your wellbeing so that you can live your life with greater clarity and meaning, wherever you are on life's journey. Our Trigger books are specifically devoted to opening up conversations about mental health and wellbeing.

Welbeck Balance and Trigger are part of the Welbeck Publishing Group – a globally recognised independent publisher based in London. Welbeck are renowned for our innovative ideas, production values and developing long-lasting content. Our books have been translated into over 30 languages in more than 60 countries around the world.

If you love books, then join the club and sign up to our newsletter for exclusive offers, extracts, author interviews and more information.

To find out more and sign up visit: **www.welbeckpublishing.com**

🐦 welbeckpublish
📷 welbeckpublish
📘 welbeckuk

Find out more about Trigger: **www.triggerhub.org**

🐦 Triggercalm
📷 Triggercalm
📘 Triggercalm